The Vintage Baking Company

Holiday Cookie
Recipe Collection

The Vintage Baking Company

Holiday Cookie

Recipe Collection

By Lisa Somerville

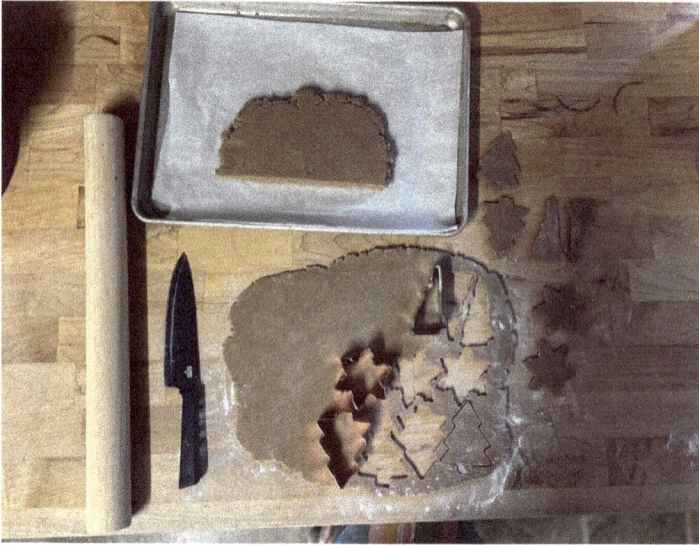

THE VINTAGE BAKING COMPANY HOLIDAY COOKIE RECIPE COLLECTION.

First edition. November 2024
Independently published v.1. Published by Lisa Somerville, 2024

ISBN: 979-8-9885570-0-5

To contact the author or to book an event, please email *cheflisasomerville@gmail.com*
For more information about the book, please visit *pastrycheflisa.com*

Dedicated to everyone in my life that has had to put up with me and my passions for baking. My family, my coworkers, students, and friends. Thanks for eating so many cookies and for putting up with my crazy ideas.

Contents:

Introduction

Iced Cookies
Sugar Cookie Dough
Gingerbread Dough
Royal Icing
American Buttercream

Shaped Cookies
Almond Horseshoes
Short Dough
White Cookies
Chocolate Walnut Clove Drops
Coconut Macaroons
Chocolate Coconut Macaroons
Pizzelles
Toasted Almond Butter Cookies
Linzer Cookies
Speculaas
Ginger Almond Thins
Peanut Butter Blossoms
Chocolate Blossoms

Contents (continued):

Drop Cookies
Chocolate Peppermint Cookies
Double Chocolate Cookies
Peanut Butter Chocolate Chip Cookies
Double Ginger Cookies
Chocolate Molasses Cookies
Rye Molasses Cookies

Biscotti
Almond Biscotti
Chocolate Nut Biscotti
Pistachio Cranberry Biscotti
Anise Biscotti
Gingerbread Biscotti

Gingerbread Hotel
in Progress

**Finished
Hotel:**

Tower roofs are gum
paste, some windows
are applied over the
royal icing paint. The
road is made of
modeling chocolate.

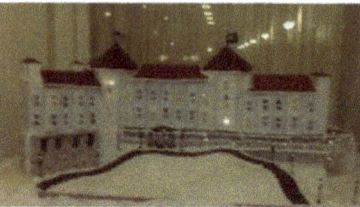

Introduction

Cookies are some of the first baked goods I remember making as a kid. I used to sit with my grandmother and roll endless amounts of White Cookies, also known as *Anginetti*, soft -yet-hard anise flavored cookies that had a sweet icing glaze and colored sprinkles. I have included a recipe here, along with a few others that were commonly made by my family.

There are countless cookies made and shared during the holiday season. I'm always amazed at the variety there are. So many people have different cookies in their orbit, whether they are made or purchased, and it just doesn't feel like the holidays without them. The recipe included for White Cookies is one shared with me by my friend Andrea. She and her mom are incredible bakers and cooks alike, and both love to share both their knowledge and bounty of food. The recipe used by my grandmother, aunt, and I over the years is at best, fickle. I think there were changes made over the years where everything was made so often, recipes were simply eyeballed instead of measured. That's the thing about cookies though; we make them time after time to bring to both casual events and milestones alike. So many families have their "signature" cookies. I will forever love hearing about family cookie traditions.

 In the bakery we get to crack open a whole special section of our cookie binder that is reserved for the holiday season. We start planning our cookie production in October. Mid-month, business gets slow, and it gives us time to get ready for the upcoming marathon of baking that will happen from mid-November straight through Easter. We start making doughs and packing them in the freezer so we can keep cookies fresh when we need them.

We spend hours upon hours decorating sugar cookies and gingerbread cookies. While we may not offer the intricately decorated cookies so many bakeries seem to be offering lately, we do try to offer a whole selection of cookies that will appease a crowd. I spend many hours considering how our cookies will be shared and gifted. I think about how far in advance someone will buy the cookies and share them- especially during Christmas week when parties are happening, skiers are hitting the slopes, and friends are gathering for dinners or coffee.

Every year on Christmas week I stress about the beloved cookie lineup: *Will there be enough of each to have a good selection? Will they stay fresh enough for a morning snack two days after Christmas?* There will be so many other items to bake and finish between December 22nd and the 24th that I simply won't have time to bake cookies those days. What was baked on the 21st will have to make do. During my planning back in October, I will consider how a chocolate peppermint cookie will be soft and chewy on the day it is baked and then be crunchy a day or two later. I appreciate the cookie both ways - I am impartial to whether a cookie is soft of crunchy, as long as it tastes delicious, and I have a cup of coffee or tea nearby. I want our customers to open a package of our cookies and really enjoy them, to look forward to them every year. I'm sure they don't always hit their mark, but I hope the forethought we put into our baking is seen and felt in something as "simple" as cookies.

Many of the recipes in this book are never made in the bakery. They are too time consuming and labor intensive to create in large amounts. All of these cookies have made into my personal cookie gift boxes over the years. I don't make large amounts of them, just enough to share with friends, neighbors, and teachers. These days I love baking with my kids, showing them special holiday cookies like the blossom cookies. Every year I have to count out and hide the kisses that will adorn the centers so we will have enough for all of the cookies. Some years we make piles of pizzelles, some years we make piles of biscotti. Every year it changes a little, but there will always be cookies.

Ingredients:

Flour
There are a huge variety of flours available in the marketplace these days. I generally prefer to use an unbleached, unbromated flour for all my baking.

All-Purpose Flour
An All-Purpose Flour is perfect for almost all cookies. Different flours serve different purposes and are categorized by the levels of protein they contain. The protein that develops in flour is called gluten. A higher protein/ high gluten flour will produce a tough, strong dough. Perfect for bagels, but not so much for cookies.

Pastry Flour
Some cookies will be best made with a pastry flour. Pastry Flour has a lower protein content, and because of that it will not develop gluten as quickly. This will help achieve a more tender crumb. Pastry flour is ideal for cookies that are shaped, cut and rerolled because of the lower protein content.

Cake Flour
Cake flour has the lowest amount of protein, which makes sense as cakes are usually soft to eat. Cake flour is also usually bleached, or heat treated, to allow it to absorb liquid better. Some of the AP Flour in supermarket is bleached as well, but that is not generally preferred for baking as it can be inconsistent from bag to bag.

If you only have a bleached AP flour on hand, it should be a fine substitute. Bromated flour should be avoided at all costs and is in fact illegal in many European countries and Canada due to Potassium Bromate's links to cancer.

Whole Grain Flour

Whole wheat, white whole wheat, and spelt flours are all very good choices for including whole grain flours in your baking. Rye is also a great grain to add to your baking but be careful switching recipes to be 100% rye flour as rye contains an enzyme called *pentosans,* which when activated through friction, can act like knives cutting through the gluten. The result is a dough that is gummy and sticky.

Whole grain flours will not only provide more nutritious products but will add flavor and texture to baked goods. There are many smaller mills popping up around the country. These mills buy grains from local farmers, which then helps to create a full circle local grain economy. If you are new to working with whole grains or regionally produced flour, start by only substituting a little at a time so you can experience the difference. Often whole grain flours absorb liquid differently, and in fact they will also absorb more water than a white flour. This can cause bakes to come out as dry and crumbly.

Butter

Not all butter is created equal. Higher quality butter contains more butterfat and is therefore more flavorful in baked goods, and flakier in pies. In baking I ALWAYS use unsalted butter. Salted butter does not have an industry standard for the amount of salt added, and therefore can vary by manufacturer. Cabot is my favorite butter brand to bake with. It is locally produced and consistent. If you have a butter you love to use, use it! I might try using a high fat butter, like Kerry Gold, for cookies where the butter flavor is the main star, such as in the Toasted Almond Butter Cookies.

Salt

I always use plain salt in baking. Plain salt is found in the supermarket aisle next to the iodized salt. It is inexpensive and has little additives and is consistent from brand to brand. Do not use iodized salt in baking, as it can contain all kinds of ingredients (including baking soda) that can affect your products. Kosher salt is an acceptable substitute, but unless you are weighing the ingredients, the grain size can be quite variable and thus affect taste.

Cocoa Powder

All of the recipes here call for simply "cocoa powder", but there are in fact, many kinds of cocoa powder. The kind of cocoa powder that should be used for the recipes in this book is Dutch-processed cocoa powder. When shopping in a store for cocoa, labels don't often have a good way of noting which cocoa has been Dutch-processed. In my local supermarket, are many varieties unsweetened cocoa powder. These cocoa powders are pale in color and very bitter in taste. There is one name brand that is labeled "Special Dark" cocoa. This is a Dutch-process cocoa, and what should be used in the recipes here. Of course, there are even higher quality cocoa powders you can find in specialty foods stores or online. Those are great too but be sure to check the ingredients label and look for the "Dutch-process" part.

Baking Powder

Sometimes bakes just don't work out right and frequently the cause is old baking powder. Baking powders can vary somewhat by brand, so some may be more resilient to aging, but the biggest issue with is moisture absorption. If your baking powder is only used once or twice a year and is stored in a box or can, it would be best to replace it for big batch bakes. Alternatively, baking powder can be stored in an airtight container. Do not store baking powder in the refrigerator, as it will be more likely to absorb moisture there.

Sugar

For recipes that call for sugar, regular granulated sugar will be fine to use.

For brown sugar, I tend to use light brown sugar. If you are using measuring cups to measure brown sugar, be sure to pack the sugar in the cup.

It is important not to arbitrarily reduce or substitute sugar in any cookie recipe. Sugar plays an important role in doughs. Sugar is hydroscopic, which means is absorbs moisture. It acts as a liquefier in dough. If sugar is reduced recipes are likely to come out dry and crumbly. Sugar substitutes can be up to 20 times sweeter than sugar. Incorrect substituting with sugar alternatives can lead to products tasting incredibly bad.

Eggs

All recipes in this book are made using large eggs. The royal icing calls for egg whites; liquid pasteurized egg whites are fine for this recipe. For the coconut macaroons, fresh egg whites must be used.

Nuts

Nuts can go bad incredibly quickly. When nuts get old, they get rancid. When rancid, nuts will taste bitter and off. Oily nuts like walnuts, pine nuts, and hazelnuts go rancid the quickest. I always buy fresh nuts for cookies, especially when gifting them.

Chocolate

Not all chocolate is created equal. My rule of thumb is as follows: if the chocolate is for mixing in, it's okay to buy the less expensive chocolate. If the chocolate is being melted, it's better to look for a better-quality product. If I am breaking large pieces to give an impressive eating experience, I'll spring for a quality chocolate bar to break up. It is always best to find the specific kind of chocolate called for in a recipe; however, I tested many of the recipes in this book with semi-sweet chocolate when the recipe called for bittersweet. There is a taste difference, but it is not significant. I find that semi-sweet chocolate is most available in supermarkets, whereas bittersweet chocolate is the workhorse of the professional kitchen. Never substitute for white chocolate, milk, chocolate, or unsweetened chocolate where it is called for, as all of these chocolates contain larger amounts of sugar (or rather contain no sugar, as for unsweetened chocolate). The difference in ingredients will have an effect on the dough that will change the consistency and eating quality of the final product.

Measuring Ingredients:

I always weigh my ingredients. I try to use the metric system whenever possible. It is much easier to scale recipes up and down, and to measure small amounts of ingredients accurately. Once you get used to weighing ingredients, your ingredient scaling will move much quicker.

Here are some helpful notes when it comes to weighing ingredients:

1 pound (1 lb) = 453g
½ Pound (0.5 lb) = 227g
¼ Pound (0.25 lb) = 114g

One box of butter = 1 pound/ 453g
One stick of butter = 0.25 pound/ 114g

1C flour = 4.5 oz / 127g
1C sugar = 6oz/ 170g
1C cocoa = 6oz/ 170g

Equipment

Having the right equipment for baking makes the process much easier. There is a lot of equipment in stores and online that might be nice to have but aren't really necessary for baking. Some cookies will be easier to make with a stand mixer. Many will be fine mixing by hand in a bowl. I used to use an electric hand mixer occasionally, but lately every time I try to use one, I find them cumbersome and messy. I don't recommend buying one for the sake of making baking easier, with the exception of making frosting.

My favorite baking tools for cookies:

- Stainless Steel Mixing bowls (multiple sizes)
- Dishers (or scoops), especially the purple and black handled ones
- Plastic Bowl Scraper
- Digital Scale
- Batter whisk
- Rubber spoonula (Rubbermaid brand is the best one)
- Kuhn Rikon Y Peeler
- Bench Knife / Dough scraper
- Half or Quarter Sheet Pans (13x18 or 9.5x13)
- Parchment Paper (buy it in precut half sheet sizes if you have space)
- Stackable cooling racks
- French Rolling Pin (JK Adams is my favorite maker)

Important Cookie Production Equipment

Dishers

Also commonly known as "scoops" are an invaluable tool for making lots of cookies. They really help keep things a consistent size. If you are investing in a disher/scoop, please research and purchase ones that are meant for a commercial purpose (like Vollrath) and have a solid handle all the way up to the round part of the scoop. All metal scoops designed for home cooks are flimsy and will break frequently.

Commercial dishers are standardized sizes, and often these sizes are arranged according to the color of the handle. They frequently have a number attached to the size like 30, 40, 16 – this number corresponds to how many scoops it will take to fill a quart container. While this number isn't super handy for cookies, it *is* handy to know that these standardized tools also have color coded handles. This is true between most brands of dishers. In the professional world, this means products can be made the same size across kitchens.

Cookie Cutters

There are so many cookie cutters on the market it can be overwhelming to choose. I find the best cutters that hold up over a long time are heavy weight metal cutters. I try to avoid the antique aluminum cutters that cover the entire piece of dough. The edges on that style of cutter are more rounded and don't make precise cuts. If you make a lot of a cookie that requires a round or fluted edge cutter, it may be best to invest in a cutter set.

Parchment paper

Parchment paper sheets can be ordered online in both small quantities and in bulk. I have a big box of parchment that is precut for half sheet pans that lives on top of my refrigerator. It is worth every penny over fighting with rolls of parchment that are bought at the supermarket.

Baking Pans

All the recipes in this book were baked on industry standard half sheet pans. They are made of light aluminum, and multiple will nest together for stacking and storage.

Oven

It's important to know the oven you are baking in. I like to say that every oven is a diva. Almost every oven will run hot or cold. Some run hot on one shelf and cold on the other. I have seen ovens that will burn the bottom of one tray of cookies, while the top tray barely bakes. Oven thermometers are helpful in determining if the oven itself runs hot or cold in general but rotating multiple trays from top to bottom and spinning them front to back will help with even cooking.

Mixing Cookie Doughs:

I tested almost all of the recipes in this book without using a mixer. The only recipes that really require a mixer are the royal icing and the coconut macaroons. I am a firm believer that good baking can be done without expensive or specialized equipment. I mainly used a stainless-steel bowl and wooden spoon or rubber spatula. If you are going to make cookies using a stand mixer, be sure to scrape down the sides of the bowl frequently to ensure all of the ingredients are being incorporated properly. The paddle attachment is designed not to scrape across the bottom of the bowl, so it never quite mixes everything in. If you are mixing by hand, a lot of the final stages of the cookie dough production are going to be stiff. There are many times when I put down my spoon and finished the dough using my hands. Using my hands allowed me to mix the dough more efficiently and put less strain on my tools. I would not recommend using an electric hand mixer for any of the recipes in this book. Hand mixers are very handy to mix recipes for baked goods like cakes but are terrible for cookie doughs.

Baker's Notes on cookie dough production:
Dough may be kept in the refrigerator for 1 week or frozen up to 1 month. Thaw frozen dough under refrigeration for 24 hours. Rolled cookie dough may need a bit of kneading when taken out from the refrigerator. It may be best to work with smaller pieces at one time to keep all the dough cold. If the dough gets soft and sticky, return it to the refrigerator until firm. This will also help the gluten relax for rerolling.

Rolled and cut cookies may also be kept unbaked and wrapped in the refrigerator or freezer. Lay unbaked cookies on a sheet pan lined with parchment paper and place cookies close together. Lay a piece of parchment over the cookies and place a second layer of cookies on top. Repeat this process for up to 3-4 layers. Wrap the entire tray with plastic wrap or with a plastic bag, the more tightly it can be wrapped, the better it will avoid freezer burn.

To bake frozen cookies, space the cookies out on a sheet pan and allow to thaw at room temperature for 30 minutes, or until soft to the touch. Proceed as if baking fresh cookie dough.

Making large amounts of cookies is easy to accomplish with a little planning ahead. Measure out the dry ingredients and store them in a container or Ziploc until needed is one technique. It's essentially making your own dry mix. Sometimes I will write the needed ingredients on the bag, so I won't have to dig out a recipe when the cookie mood strikes. Another is to make the cookie dough, scoop it out with a standard size disher, and freeze the dough until it is needed. That way you can have a whole variety of cookies to choose from and bake off just what you need at one time.

Equipment Resources:

Webstaurauntstore.com - Has just about everything you can think of for restaurant equipment. You don't always have to order in bulk.

King Arthur Baking Company – Lots of items available online (plenty of things you don't need too…) but their store is in Norwich, VT and worth a visit.

Independent Restaurant Supply – Two locations: Portsmouth, NH and Portland, ME. You don't need to be a professional to shop in these stores and the prices are much more reasonable than other kitchen stores.

JK Adams: A wood producer in VT that makes my favorite French rolling pins. They also make great cutting boards.

Cakedeco.com - If you really want a deep dive in specialty baking equipment

Evilcakegenius.com – For all kinds of great equipment to take a deep dive into decorated sugar cookies and cakes

Iced Cookies

Iced Cookies have come to define fancy cookies year-round, not just at the holidays. At the bakery, we only get the chance to work on iced cookies at the holiday season. We will work on them a couple of hours at a time in stages. We make the dough and freeze it in stages, the cookies get rolled and cut in stages, they get baked and iced in stages too. Baking huge amounts of cookies start to finish can get overwhelming quickly. Working a little at a time helps keep the experience fun and exciting.
Every year I get incredible excited about gingerbread. I rarely get to spend the hours I crave making intricate decorations anymore. I haven't gotten to do that really since I worked at the Mount Washington Hotel where we made huge displays every year. The displays would take up an 8 foot by 10 foot board. The year we built a gingerbread replica of the hotel it took 8 people to carry it from the bakery to the main lobby. Quite a feat!

Rolled Sugar Cookies

There are as many variations of sugar cookies as there are bakers who make them. I have always liked these cookies because they are crunchy, but not *too* crunchy. Using cake flour is important so that the cookies don't get tough. This dough can be rerolled many times, but it will likely need time to chill in the refrigerator in between rolling. These cookies will puff up and spread a bit when baking.

Ingredient	Home	Metric
Butter, soft	1C (2 sticks)	227g
Sugar	1 1/2 C	283g
Egg	1 ea	50g
Milk	1/4 C	60g
Vanilla Extract	1 1/2 t	7g
Cake flour	4 1/2 C	600g
Baking powder	4t	14g
Salt	1t	5g

Preheat oven to 350F
Yield will vary depending on the cookie size

Method
Making the dough:
Measure dry ingredients and mix just to combine. Set aside.
In a mixer fitted with the paddle attachment, cream the butter and sugar together until it looks fluffy.
Add egg, mix to combine.
Combine the milk and vanilla extract, add to butter mixture. It may look curdled and lumpy, this is okay.
Add dry ingredients and mix until a dough forms.
Flatten the dough into a disk
Wrap the dough in plastic wrap and chill until firm.

Making Cookies:
Preheat oven to 350F
Roll the dough out to about a ¼ inch thickness
(It may help to flour your work surface lightly)
Cut into desired shapes and arrange onto a cookie sheet
Bake cookies for about 8-10 minutes or until the edges are
just barely browned
Allow to fully cool if icing.

Gingerbread Dough

I have used this dough in many ways over many years. It produces a warm colored gingerbread, not one that is a deep chocolatey brown. If you'd like a gingerbread that has heavier amounts of spices, feel free to add more. For cookies use butter instead of margarine. The role of margarine is to keep the cost down, but also the

Ingredient	Home	Metric	Large Batch
Margarine or butter	1 C (2 sticks)	212g	425g
Sugar	1C	212g	425g
Corn syrup	¾ C	255g	509
Milk	6T	80g	¾ C
Flour	5 1/3 C	680g	1359g
Baking soda	1 ½ t	7g	1T
Cinnamon	2T	16g	¼ C
Cloves	1T	8g	2T
Ginger	1T	5g	2T

margarine is less likely to shrink in the oven. Keeping exact sizes will help with baking gingerbread house parts.

Bake 350 F
Yield will vary based on cutter size/ shape

To Make the Dough:
Method
Heat margarine, sugar, corn syrup, and milk in a saucepan over medium heat
Heat until margarine is just melted
DO NOT OVERHEAT!!!

Place butter or margarine mixture in a bowl of a mixer fitted with a paddle attachment
Add dry ingredients
Mix until incorporated
Line a sheet pan with parchment, sprinkle with flour
Flatten dough into the sheet pan and refrigerate overnight, covered

To Shape Cookies:
Roll chilled dough on a lightly floured surface to 1/8"-1/4" thickness. Dip the cookie cutter in flour, then cut your shape. Arrange on a sheet pan lined with parchment paper.

To Shape Houses:
Have your template ready
Work with chilled dough, but not the entire batch of dough at once.
Roll the dough to ¼ " thick on a piece of parchment.
Remove the scraps but try not to disturb the house shape itself. If cutting windows or doors, cut the shape out but **don't remove it**. You'll remove it part way through baking.

Pro Tip: To assemble gingerbread houses, sand uneven edges with sandpaper or a Dremel tool

For Baking:
You'll need sheet pans lined with parchment and extra pieces of parchment if you are rolling out houses.
Preheat the oven to 375F
Both cookies and houses should be baked to an even brownness to ensure a crispy cookie.

Special Equipment for Gingerbread House construction
When making gingerbread houses, especially large ones, it is important to have a strong and sturdy base. Large structures should be supported by a wooden base. Smaller ones can be supported by cardboard, I prefer to use cardboard drums made for cakes. They have a smaller tendency to buckle and fold when carrying.
I also find using some specialized equipment like plastic disposable piping bags helpful when decorating details. A good set of piping tips will be helpful if you are piping clapboard siding or decorative shells over the seams.
There are whole books and websites dedicated to assembling gingerbread houses. A lot of home bakers use royal icing to assemble, but it takes many hours to dry hard. Using caramel as an assembly glue is very fast and strong. If you expect to want to display the house for longer than a week or two, assemble the house with Isomalt instead of sugar. Isomalt is a humidity resistant sugar that will not melt over time.
Gingerbread house templates are also available online. A photocopier can help enlarge the size to make the house bigger. I like to trace the paper onto a sturdier material like the paper a cake or cereal box is made out of. Once

your template is cut out, you can tape it together to be sure all of the pieces fit together.

The dough pieces used for larger houses will take up most of a sheet pan. It will be important to keep the dough cold so that it will not shrink when baking. If you don't have room in your fridge or freezer and it is below 40F outside, you could chill the dough for 20-30 minutes, covered, outside.

Royal Icing

There are two rules of thumb about royal icing that are at odds with each other. Either make a small batch and use up everything or make up a large batch so there will be enough for the project. I have chosen to list a larger batch size, which is perfect for making gingerbread houses or large amounts of cookies. My usual procedure is to make a thicker icing that I can a bit of water to if I need it thinner.

Ingredient	Home	Metric
Egg whites	6 ea	300g
Confectioner's sugar, sifted	1ea 2# bag	1132g
Cream of tartar	¼ t	1-2g

Preheat oven to 350F
Yield

Method
Pour egg whites into bowl of a mixer fitted with a paddle attachment
Gradually add powdered sugar, mixing on low speed in between additions until the mixture is smooth and looks pasty.
Mix the icing on medium to high speed to reach the desired consistency
For piping, mix the icing until it is light and fluffy and holds a sharp point then the paddle is lifted from the bowl of icing.

For flooding (this is the covering of the cookie with icing) use a thinner icing.

If you are flooding a cookie with royal icing, you'll need a thicker icing piped along the edges so that the icing doesn't run over the sides. It is best to let the outline icing harden for a few hours or overnight before filling the center.

American Style Buttercream

This is a great basic frosting for cakes and cupcakes, but it also works really well for frosting sugar cookies.

Ingredient	Home	Metric
Butter, soft	1 C (2 sticks)	453g
Confectioner's Sugar	4 ½ C	566g
Milk	¼ C	60g
Vanilla extract	1 ½ t	7g

Method

Beat butter and confectioner's sugar in a mixer with a paddle until light and fluffy
Combine milk mixture and vanilla
Slowly pour milk mixture into butter mixture ad mixer is running on low speed

For icing sugar cookies:
Mix the butter and sugar while the butter is still cold and substitute heavy cream for the half and half.

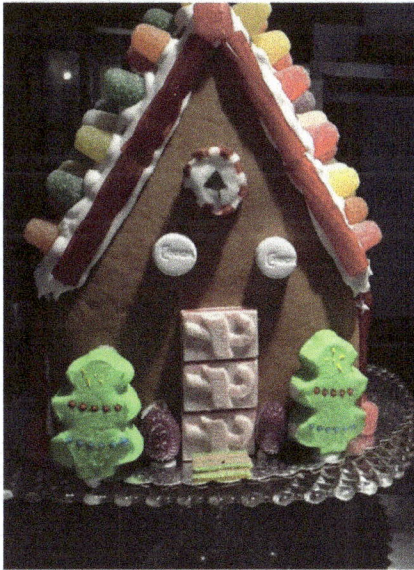

Shaped Cookies

When I think about shaped cookies, I think about styles of cookies that require a little more organization and forethought than a scooped cookie. The cookies in this section all have some sort of shaping involved in their makeup. Much of the doughs require refrigeration before it can be baked. The advantage of shaped cookies is that they can be stored in the freezer until needed. For example, the toasted almond cookies are shaped into a log before being sliced and baked. The logs can be stored in the freezer for months, and taken out, thawed overnight in a refrigerator, sliced, and baked any time.

Almond Horseshoes

These cookies have been a long time favorite at the bakery, but we stopped making them when almond paste got really expensive, and the cookies had a hard time being handled without breaking. We bring them back every holiday season, sometimes full size, sometimes in a mini size.

Ingredient	Home	Metric
Almond paste	16 oz	453g
Sugar	1 1/3 C	266g
Egg whites	2 ea	70g
Vanilla Extract	½ t	2g
Almond Extract	½ t	2g
Sliced Almonds	As needed	

Preheat oven to 350F
Yield about 16 cookies

Method

To Make the Dough:
In a mixer fitted with a paddle attachment, mix sugar and almond paste until the mixture looks like crumbs.
Add egg whites and extracts. Continue mixing on low speed until the mixture forms a paste.
Increase the speed to medium-high and beat until the mixture is visibly lighter in color.
Scoop the dough with a spoon or a disher that has a black handle. If a spoon was used, shape the dough into a round-ish shape before chilling

Chill for 3 hours or overnight.
At this point the dough can be refrigerated for up to a
week or frozen for up to a month.

To Bake:
Preheat the oven to 350F
Prepare a cookie sheet by lining it with parchment paper.
Prepare a space to roll the dough (either a space on the
counter or on a tray or large, flat plate)
Shape the dough by rolling into a rope shape while rolling
in almonds. It should be about 5 inches when done. They
should be well coated in the sliced almonds.
Transfer the cookies to the prepared cookie sheet, shaping
them into a horseshoe shape.

Bake for about 12-18 minutes or until the cookies are a
light golden brown. It will help the cookies brown evenly if
the try is spun halfway through baking.
Let them cool completely on the cookie sheet and transfer
carefully to store.

Short Dough Cookies

This dough is one that can be rolled out for tart shells, shaped into a log for traditional refrigerator cookies, and more. I like to use it for a quick and easy cookie at the holidays. These cookies go by many names, and I've encountered quite a few variations over the years. The important part is to roll the cookies in powdered sugar once before baking, and again after they have been baked and cooled.

Ingredient	Home	Metric
Flour	4 C	565g
Sugar	2/3 C	174g
Baking powder	½ t	3g
Butter, cold, cubed	3 sticks + 2T	368g
Eggs	1 ea	56g
Milk	4t	21g
Chopped nuts	2C	127g
Powdered sugar for rolling		

Preheat oven to 350F
Yield about 36 cookies

Method

Mix flour, sugar, and baking powder in mixer with a paddle attachment until combined
Add butter and mix until sandy looking
Combine eggs and milk, add to flour mixture all at once
Mix on low speed until a smooth dough forms.
Add your choice of chopped nuts.

Once the nuts have been incorporated, form the dough into balls the size of a small whole walnut. If using a disher type scoop, I like to use a black handled disher.
Prepare a wide shallow container (a 9x13 baking pan is good) with sifted powdered sugar.
Roll the cookies in the powdered sugar and arrange them on a sheet tray lined with parchment paper.
Bake the cookies for about 14-16 minutes or until they puff up a little and brown a little on the edges.
Once completely cooled, roll the cookies in the powdered sugar a second time.

Baker's Notes:
Here are popular variation names of these cookies I have heard of:
-Blanched Sliced Almonds: Greek Wedding Cookies
-Walnuts: Mexican Wedding Biscuits
-Pecans: Russian Tea Biscuits

White Cookies

These cookies are commonly referred to as *Anginetti* cookies. It seems every Italian family in the Merrimack Valley area of Massachusetts had their own recipe for these cookies growing up. We always made them with anise extract, but if you don't like anise, you could easily substitute lemon or vanilla. Don't skip on the glaze, it is an important part of these cookies. It gives them a kind of creamy topping to an otherwise drier dough. Adding extract to the glaze helps give a flavor boost too.

If you'd like to freeze these cookies for sharing, freeze them baked and unglazed.

Ingredient	Home	Metric
Flour	2C	280g
Baking powder	2t	7g
Salt	pinch	2g
Eggs	2	100g
Butter, melted and cooled	6T	85g
Sugar	½ C	100g
Anise extract	1t	5g
Vanilla extract	1t	5g

Colorful Nonpareils or colored sanding sugar for garnish

Preheat oven to 350°F
Yield 20 cookies

Method

In a bowl, stir together eggs, butter, sugar, and extracts.
Add the flour, baking powder, and salt
Stir together to make a dough. It may be a bit sticky.
Pinch off small amounts, about 1" in diameter, and roll into a ball with the palms of your hands (kind of like shaping a meatball).

Place cookies on a parchment lined sheet pan.

Bake 8-10 minutes until the bottom edges just barely turn brown. It is okay for the main part of the cookie to stay a blonde color.

Let cool.

Once cool, glaze with anise glaze. Garnish with colorful nonpareils or colored sanding sugar as desired.

Chocolate Clove Drops

These cookies are sometimes also known as *Totos*. I remember my Aunt Emma making them from time to time when I was a kid. They were so different from the white cookies my grandmother and I made together. I love the combination of clove and chocolate in these cookies, even though I am not generally a fan of clove. I also love the crunch that the walnuts add to the cookie. Just be sure to chop them finely so they mix thoroughly with the dough. If you'd like to freeze these cookies for sharing, freeze them baked and unglazed.

Ingredient	Home	Metric
Flour	2 ½ C	630g
Cocoa powder	¼ C	22g
Baking powder	3t	11g
Baking soda	½ t	2g
Ground cloves	1t	8g
Ground nutmeg	½ t	3g
Ground cinnamon	½ t	3g
Sugar	¾ C	150g
Milk	½ C	121g
Oil	½ C	112g
Finely chopped walnuts (optional)	¾ C	85g

Preheat oven to 350°F
Yields 30-32 cookies

Method

In a bowl, whisk together the egg, milk, oil, and sugar.
In a separate bowl measure flour, cocoa, baking powder, baking soda, and spices.
Add the dry ingredients to the wet ones, stirring to combine (add the walnuts now too if you are using them).

It will make a thick dough. You may need to use your hands a bit to knead the dough together but be careful not to get carried away and overmix.

Pinch the dough and shape it into a ball about 1" in diameter.

Place onto a sheet pan lined with parchment paper, spacing them evenly.

Bake for 8-10 minutes, or until they feel firm when you gently press the tops.

When cool, glaze with chocolate glaze.

Glazes

Anise Glaze

Ingredient	Home	Metric
Confectioner's sugar	2C	230g
Anise extract	1t	5g
Milk, warmed	3-4T	45-60g

Place the confectioner's sugar, anise extract, and water into a bowl. Whisk together to combine.

Dip the tops of the cookies into the glaze and place on a cooling rack. Sprinkle with colored nonpareils while still wet. Allow to dry for a while, then move to an airtight container for storage.

Chocolate Glaze

Ingredient	Home	Metric
Confectioner's sugar	1 ½ C	173g
Cocoa powder	¼ C	23g
Milk, warmed slightly	6T	90g

Place confectioner's sugar, cocoa, and milk in a bowl. Whisk together to combine.

Dip the tops of the cookies into the glaze and place on a cooling rack. Allow to dry for a while, then move to an airtight container for storage.

Pizzelles

Pizzelles are a cookie that I make almost exclusively at the holidays. I don't know why I don't think of them at other times of the year, they are easy to make and quick and fun to bake with kids. I have tried to make them at the bakery to sell a few times, but the fact that I can only make two at a time coupled with the need to stand watch at the iron make the task a chore. Feel free to substitute the butter with a vegetable oil if you prefer. The batter will be softer, and it will spread more easily. I prefer to use butter because I like the taste, and the fact that I can scoop the dough ahead of time if needed. If you are making these to give as gifts, I'd suggest making a double batch. It helps when your family get nosy about the good smells and inevitably swipe one or two as a snack.

Ingredient	Home	Metric
Eggs	3	150g
Sugar	¾ C	150g
Butter, melted and cooled	½ C (1 stick)	114g
Anise extract	1 T	14g
Flour	1 ¾ C	245g
Baking powder	2 t	7g

Preheat electric pizzelle iron before making up the dough to be sure it will be thoroughly heated when the batter is ready.

Yield about 22 cookies

Method

In a bowl, whisk together the eggs and sugar until thick and smooth.

Stir in the melted butter and anise extract.
In a separate bowl, combine the flour and baking powder.
Add the flour mixture to the egg mixture.
The dough will be soft at first and will set up quickly. Note that if oil was substituted for butter, it will not set up, but will remain a bit runny.

To cook, scoop using a purple handled scoop (or use a spoon), place the dough onto the pizzelle iron.
Close the iron and bake according to the manufacturer's directions.

Toasted Almond Butter Cookies

Sometimes I skim over a recipe too fast and miss something. I get really excited to get going and seem to miss part of the instructions. This cookie recipe originally appeared in *The Greens*, a cookbook by Deborah Madison. What I missed when I first made these was an instruction to finely grind the almonds before adding them to the dough. I only realized this difference when double checking the original recipe against the one I had been using for many years. You can grind the almonds and make the dough smooth if you like, but I like seeing the toasted flecks of almond throughout.

Ingredient	Home	Metric
Sliced almonds, toasted	3/4 C	65g
Butter, softened	2 sticks	228g
Powdered sugar	¾ C	86g
Salt	½ t	3g
Almond Extract	½ t	2g
Vanilla Extract	¾ t	3g
Flour	2C	280g

Additional powdered sugar for dusting

Preheat oven to 350F
Yield about 75 cookies

Method

Cream the butter and sugar.
Add the salt and extracts and mix until combined.
Stir in the almonds.
Add the flour and mix to form a smooth dough.
If mixing by hand, the dough will be very stiff. Be prepared to mix the final bit with your hands if needed.

Shape the dough into 1 to 1 ½ inch logs and wrap in plastic and place in the refrigerator to chill.

When ready to bake, slice the logs into ¼ inch coins and bake about 8 min or until the tops are just barely turning a golden brown. Remove from oven and dust with confectioner's sugar while still warm.

Linzer Cookies

These were some of the first fancy cookies I was ever introduced to. I was in Colorado working for Eastern Mountain Sports (an outdoor retail company), and my coworker Karen brought these cookies in. These were her holiday tradition cookie. They are a little finicky and take patience but it's so worth it. The best part is that the cookies get better after a couple of days.

Ingredient	Home	Metric
Butter, soft	3 sticks	340g
Sugar	1C	200g
Eggs	1 ea	50g
Egg yolks	1 ea	15g
Lemon zest	1t	2g
Vanilla	½ t	2g
Finely ground almonds	4C	340g
Cake flour	3 ½ C	465g
Baking powder	1t	4g
Cinnamon	1 ¾ t	5g
Raspberry preserves as needed		
Powdered sugar for dusting		

Preheat oven to 350F
Yield about 74 finished cookies when cut with a 2" round cutter

Method
Cream butter and sugar in mixer fitted with a paddle attachment.
Add egg, yolk, lemon, and vanilla and mix until combined.
Add the ground nuts.
In a separate bowl, combine flour, cinnamon, baking powder

Add the dry ingredients to egg mixture and mix on low speed to form a dough.

Turn the dough out onto a piece of plastic wrap or parchment paper and press into a disk about ½ inch thick. Chill the dough for several hours or overnight.

Remove the dough from the refrigerator and knead it slightly to break up the dough.

Work with ¼ to ½ of the dough at a time to avoid it becoming too soft. If the dough becomes soft and sticky, return it to the refrigerator long enough for it to be firm.

Lightly flour the worksurface and roll the dough to be about ¼ "thick.

Cut the dough with a round or fluted cutter and transfer to a parchment lined sheet pan.

The cookies will rise and spread a little.

Using a smaller cutter, cut a "window" out of half of the cookies.

Bake the cookies for about 8 minutes until they are just barely browned.

Once cool, spread a little raspberry preserves onto each bottom cookie and top with the cookies with a "window" to make a sandwich cookie.

Sift powdered sugar over the cookies.

Speculaas Cookies

These Dutch favorites came to us by a former baker, Cate. Speculaas were her favorite holiday cookies to make, and we have made them every year since she introduced us to them. They are a welcome snappy, crunchy cookie in a sea of soft and chewy ones. The dough is freezable, as are the rolled and cut cookies. The baked cookies hold for at least a week. They may last longer, but I've never made enough to find out.

Note: When Cate first made these I kept calling them "Speculoos" instead of "Speculaas". We looked it up and it tuns out that "Speculoos" Cookies are made with only one kind of spice, whereas "Speculaas" are made from a blend of spices.

Speculaas Spice Mix

8 parts cinnamon
2 parts nutmeg
2 parts cloves
1 part white pepper
1 part ginger
1 part cardamom

Cookie Dough

Ingredient	Home	Metric
Unsalted butter, soft	2 sticks	227g
Sugar	1C	200g
Brown Sugar	1 ¼ C	g
Eggs	2	100g
Vanilla Extract	2T	28g
Flour	3½ C	453g
Baking soda	2t	g
Salt	1t	6g
Spice Mix	3T	60g

Bake 350 F
Yield will vary based on cutter size/ shape

Method
Place the flour, baking soda, salt and spice mix in a bowl and whisk to combine.
Set aside.
In another bowl, cream the butter and sugars together until light.
Add the eggs and the vanilla extract.
Add the flour mixture and stir to combine.

Place the dough onto a parchment lined sheet pan or tray.
Press the dough down to make a disk to be about ½ "thick.
Cover the dough with plastic wrap to keep it from drying out.
Chill the dough until firm, several hours or overnight.

Roll the dough to about ¼" thick and cut into desired shapes.

Bake 8-10 minutes.

Dough scraps may be rerolled. Chill in between rolling if the dough feels too soft and sticky.

Ginger Almond Thins

These cookies were the first cookie recipe I ever saw in a magazine and said, "I have to save this." It was the winning recipe in a cookie recipe contest put on my *Martha Stewart Living* back in 1997. In the time since I have made my own modifications to the original. The original called for the addition of crystallized ginger, which I always find makes the cookies break when you cut them. Cut them with a sharp chef's knife for the best results. If they don't come out perfectly rectangular, that's okay. They'll still taste incredible.

Ingredient	Home	Metric
Unsalted Butter, soft	(1C) 2 sticks	228g
Molasses	½ C	168g
Lemon extract	1t	5g
Vanilla Extract	1t	5g
Lemon zest	2t	4g
Flour	3 ½ C	490g
Sugar	1C	200g
Ginger, ground	1T	15g
Baking soda	1t	5g
Cinnamon	1t	5g
Sliced Almonds, toasted	1C	86g

Bake 350 F
Yield about 80 cookies

Method

In a bowl, combine the soft butter, molasses, extracts, and lemon zest.
Add the cinnamon, baking soda, and ginger and stir until combined.
Add the sugar and stir until combined.

Add the flour and stir using to a wooden spoon. The dough will be very stiff.
Stir in the almonds.

Divide the dough in half and place it on two sections of plastic wrap that have been spread out on the counter.

Shape each dough into a rectangle about 3 inches by 6 inches. Press the top of the rectangle flat. It should be about 1 ½ "high.

Wrap the dough tightly and chill for several hours or overnight. It should be very firm.

Using a sharp chef's knife, slice the cookies into 1/8" slices.

Arrange the cookies on a parchment lined sheet pan. Be sure to leave room between the cookies because they will expand some.

Bake about 8-10 minutes, just until the edges begin to darken.

Peanut Butter Blossoms

A lot of people grow up with these cookies around the holidays, but I didn't make these until I had kids. I prefer to use dark chocolate kisses if I am going to be eating these cookies, but most people (my kids included) prefer the milk chocolate version.

Ingredient	Home	Metric
Flour	3 ½ C	516g
Baking soda	2t	10g
Salt	1t	7g
Butter, unsalted	2 sticks	228g
Peanut butter	1C	260g
Sugar	1C	200g
Brown Sugar	1C	220g
Eggs	2	100g
Milk	2T	24g
Vanilla	2t	6g
Chocolate Kisses	50	

Bake 350 F
Yield about 50 cookies

Method

Combine the flour, salt, and baking soda. Set aside.
In a mixer fitted with a paddle attachment, cream the butter and sugar until light.
Add the eggs and mix on low speed until incorporated.
Add the peanut butter and mix until combined.
Add the milk and vanilla extract and mix until combined.
Scrape down the sides of the bowl and the paddle to ensure everything is mixed thoroughly.
Add the dry ingredients and mix on low speed.

Scoop the dough with a purple handled disher or shape the dough into rounds about 1 ½" in diameter.

Place the sugar for rolling in a wide shallow container like a pie pan.

Roll the rounds in sugar to coat.

Arrange on a parchment lined sheet pan.

Bake 12-14 minutes or until the cookies have spread and are puffy.

Remove the pan from the oven and press a kiss candy into the center of each cookie, pressing down on the middle.

Chocolate Blossoms

These cookies came about because I wanted to make a chocolate peppermint cookie that had a more intense flavor than the chocolate peppermint drop cookies I had made previously. Only during the holiday season, Hershey's produces a wide variety of different flavors for their Kisses® Candies. Using the peppermint candy cane kisses with a chocolatey cookie reminds me of peppermint bark, one of my all-time favorite candies at Christmastime. If you want to make these cookies in other times of the year, they can easily be made into a chocolate peanut butter blossom by using a mini peanut butter cup, or simply double down on the chocolate with a small piece of your favorite chocolate candy. I like to use Dove Promises.

Ingredient	Home	Metric
Flour	1 1/2 C	210g
Cocoa powder	3/4 C	67g
Salt	1/2 t	3g
Baking soda	3/4 t	4g
Baking powder	1/2 t	2g
Unsalted butter, softened	3/4 C (1 ½ sticks)	170g
Sugar	1 C	200g
Egg	1 ea	50g
Milk	2 T	30g
Vanilla extract	1 T	15g
Sugar for rolling	1 C	100g
Peppermint Kiss candy	30	

Bake 350 F
Yield 30 cookies

Method

Combine the flour, cocoa, salt, baking soda, and baking powder baking powder. Set aside.

In a mixer fitted with a paddle attachment, cream the butter and sugar until light.

Add the egg and mix on low speed until incorporated.

Add the milk and vanilla extract and mix until combined.

Scrape down the sides of the bowl and the paddle to ensure everything is mixed thoroughly.

Add the dry ingredients and mix on low speed.

Shape the dough into rounds about 1 ½" in diameter.

Place the sugar for rolling in a wide shallow container like a pie pan.

Roll the rounds in sugar to coat.

Arrange on a parchment lined sheet pan.

Bake 8 minutes or until the cookies have spread and are puffy.

Remove the pan from the oven and press a kiss candy into the center of each cookie, pressing down on the middle.

Drop Cookies

Drop cookies are one of my favorite things to make, ever. There are endless varieties to make. I never really get tired of making (and snacking on) cookies. When I worked in hotels we made heaps of cookie dough that would get scooped into teeny tiny cookies for afternoon tea. In the bakery we make giant cookies. Our batches make upwards over 100 of these giant cookies at a time.

Chocolate Peppermint Cookies

These are our original holiday cookie. We have made these cookies at the holidays every year we have been open. Sometimes I make up a batch at other times of the year just so I can eat one, but they never seem to stay on the rotation. One year I tried to add chopped candy canes to the dough to make it extra minty, but the sugar in the candy made the whole cookie spread very thinly and it was crunchy, not chewy. These cookies will be chewy when first baked, and crunchy a couple of days later. I like them both ways- the chewy ones are more like a chocolate chip cookie, and the crunchy one reminds me of a thin minty cookie.

Ingredient	Home	Metric
Unsalted butter, soft	12 T (1 ½ sticks)	170g
Brown sugar	½ C	100g
Sugar	½ C	100g
Eggs	1 ea	50g
Vanilla Extract	1t	5g
Peppermint Extract	1t	5g
Flour	1 ½ C	210g
Dutch Process Cocoa	¼ C	45g
Baking soda	1t	4g
Salt	1t	3g
Chocolate chips	1C	170g

Preheat oven to 350F
Yield 26 cookies

Method

In a bowl, sift the cocoa powder. Add the flour, baking soda, and salt and whisk to combine. Set aside.
Cream butter and sugars until light.

Add egg, beating well after adding.
Add in extracts, stir to combine.
Add remaining dry ingredients, stir until combined.
Add chocolate chunks and mix to incorporate.
Scoop the dough with a purple handled disher or spoon the dough into about tablespoon sized balls.
Place the cookies on a parchment lined sheet pan.
Bake 10-12 minutes

Double Chocolate Cookies

This recipe came to us from the Balsam's Hotel thanks to a friend that was a former apprentice there. I like them because they have a different texture than the chocolate peppermint cookies. They have a lighter, more cakey texture. You can sub the chocolate chips for a host of other options like white chocolate, peanut butter, or even butterscotch. If you prefer a soft cookie, bake these cookies a little less rather than a little more. If you like a crunchy cookie better, leave them in for the full time suggested.

Ingredient	Home	Metric
Unsalted butter, soft	10T (1 stick plus 2T)	143g
Brown Sugar	1C +2T	225g
Eggs	2	100g
Vanilla Extract	1t	5g
Flour	2C	280g
Cocoa powder	½ C	45g
Baking soda	¼ t	2g
Salt	½ t	3g
Chocolate Chunks	1 ½ C	255g

Preheat oven to 375F
Yield about 24 cookies

Method
In a bowl, whisk together the flour and the cocoa powder. Set aside.
In a separate bowl, cream the butter and sugar.
Add eggs and mix until smooth.
Add the baking soda and salt, stir until combined.
Add the flour mixture and mix until smooth.
Add the chocolate chunks.

Scoop with a black handled disher or spoon the dough into about tablespoon sized balls.
Place the cookies on a parchment lined sheet pan.
Bake 10-12 minutes.

Peanut Butter Chocolate Chunk Cookies

I love a peanut butter cookie, but I always want there to be *something more*. Adding chocolate chunks to these cookies is a perfect way to make the cookie richer, but not too rich. I also like to guild the Lilly with massive shards of chocolate and a pinch of fancy flaky sea salt. My favorite chocolate bar to use is by Lindt. Sometimes I use dark chocolate, and sometimes I use milk chocolate, it's baker's choice what to use.

Ingredient	Home	Metric
Butter	1 stick	114g
Brown sugar	¾ C	150g
Sugar	1/3 C	67g
Eggs	2	100g
Vanilla extract	1t	5g
Peanut butter	½ C	128g
Flour	1 ¼ C	175g
Baking powder	½ t	2g
Salt	½ t	3g
Semi-sweet chips	1 C	170g
Good quality chocolate	1 bar	114g
Maldon Sea Salt for garnish		

Preheat the oven to 350 F
Yield about 24 Cookies

Method
Cream butter and sugars
Add eggs and mix until smooth
Add peanut butter and mix to combine
Add the baking powder and salt, stir until combined
Add the flour and mix until smooth
Add the chocolate chips

Scoop with a purple handled scoop or spoon the dough into about tablespoon sized balls.
Roughly chop the chocolate bar.
Place the chocolate and put it int the cookies vertically so they look spiky
Sprinkle a pinch of Maldon Sea salt on the top of each cookie.
Place the cookies on a parchment lined sheet pan.
Bake 10-12 minutes

Double Ginger Cookies

When we first opened the bakery these were a bakery staple. I like the chunks of crystallized ginger as an added zing. We stopped making them only because one day we ran out of crystallized ginger. We adjusted the spices and made molasses cookies instead, and they have been selling great ever since. I still make these at the holidays though.

Ingredient	Home	Metric
Butter, softened	2 sticks	228g
Sugar	1 1/3 C	266g
Molasses	1/3 C	112g
Eggs	2	100g
Flour	3C	420g
Ground Ginger	1T + 2t	25g
Baking soda	1 ¼ t	6g
Salt	½ t	3g
Crystallized ginger	1C	184g
Granulated sugar for rolling		

Preheat the oven 375F
Yield about 32 cookies

Method

Finely chop the crystallized ginger. Set aside.
Cream butter and sugar.
Add the molasses and mix to combine.
Add eggs and mix to combine.
Add the ginger, baking soda, and salt.
Add the flour and mix until evenly combined.
Stir in the crystallized ginger.

Scoop or spoon the dough into about tablespoon sized balls.
Roll in sugar and place on a parchment lined sheet pan.

Bake 12-14 minutes.
The surface will crack but will look wet when done.

Chocolate Molasses Cookies

I grew up with a cookie called a "Dutch Cocoa Cookie" from a company called "Archway". The cookies came from the supermarket and were soft and chewy and just heaven. You can still buy them, but the recipe has changed with the addition of palm kernel oil. This is the closest reproduction I have been able to make.

Ingredient	Home	Metric
Butter, melted	12T (1 ½ sticks)	170g
Brown sugar	½ C	100g
Sugar	1/3C	67g
Salt	½ t	3g
Baking soda	2t	10g
Egg	1	50g
Vanilla extract	1t	5g
Molasses	1/3 C	112g
Flour	2C	280g
Cocoa powder	1/3 C	178g
Granulated sugar for rolling		

Preheat the oven to 350 F
Yield about 21 cookies

In a bowl, combine the flour, cocoa, and baking soda. Set aside.
In a separate bowl, stir together the melted butter, brown sugar, and sugar
Add the molasses and salt. Stir to combine.
Stir in the egg and vanilla extract.
Stir in the flour mixture, mix until fully combined.
The dough will be soft.
Scoop with a purple handled disher or spoon the dough into about tablespoon sized balls.

Chill for 1 hour.
Round the cookie dough as needed.
Roll the cookies in sugar and place on a parchment lined sheet pan.
Bake 8-12 minutes until puffy and cracked looking.
Bake an additional 3-5 minutes for a crunchy cookie.

Rye Molasses Cookies

These cookies were developed by one of my baking classes that I teach at Lakes Region Community College in Laconia, NH. In the class, I challenged the students to introduce and increase whole grains into everyday baking. We substituted rye flour for half of the white flour and the results were a delicious, chewy, and more flavorful cookie. It was so good I added it to the holiday cookie lineup starting in 2022.

Ingredient	Home	Metric
Butter, soft	2 sticks	228g
Sugar	1 1/3 C	267g
Molasses	1/3 C	112g
Eggs	2 ea.	100g
Flour	1 ½ C	210g
Rye Flour	1 ½ C	210g
Baking Soda	1 ¼ t	6g
Ginger	¾ t	4g
Cloves	¼ t	2g
Cinnamon	¾ t	6g
Salt	½ t	3g
Sugar for rolling		

Preheat oven to 375°F
Yield about 28 cookies

Method
In a bowl, stir together the dry ingredients (flour, spices, baking powder, baking soda, salt) to combine.
Cream the butter and sugar until pale and fluffy looking.
Add the eggs and mix until light.
Add the dry ingredients and mix to combine.

Scoop the dough with a black handled scoop or spoon the dough into ping pong sized pieces.

Chill the scooped cookies about 1 hour.

Roll the cookies in sugar and place on a parchment lined sheet pan. Gently press down on the top of each cookie to flatten it slightly.

Bake 8-12 minutes until puffy and cracked looking.

Oatmeal Cranberry Nut Cookies

I was handed this recipe by chef Mark Prince back in 2004 when I was the baker at the Eagle Mountain House. It was one of his favorites and I soon learned why. I like the variety away from the traditional oatmeal raisin cookie for a holiday treat. Dried cranberries add a tart flavor, and the walnuts add a nice crunch. If you are feeling fancy, substitute chopped dried cherries for the cranberries and hazelnuts for the walnuts.

Ingredient	Home	Metric
Unsalted butter, softened	2 Sticks (1C)	228g
Brown sugar	1C	200g
Sugar	½ C	100g
Eggs	2 ea.	100g
Vanilla	1t	5g
Flour	1 ½ C	210g
Salt	1t	5g
Baking soda	1t	5g
Rolled Oats	2C	178g
Dried cranberries	1 C	170g
Chopped walnuts	1C	114g

Preheat oven to 375°F
Yield about 30 cookies

Method
Cream the butter and sugar until light.
Add the eggs and mix until blended.
Add the baking powder, baking soda, and vanilla extract. Stir to combine.
Add the oats.
Add the flour and mix until it becomes a smooth dough.

Mix in the walnuts and cranberries.
Scoop the dough with a black handled scoop or spoon the dough into ping pong sized pieces.

Bake 8-12 minutes.

Volcano Cookies

When I first worked in Jackson in 1997, there was a bakery called *As You Like It* and they were well known for many baked goods, but especially their chocolate crinkle cookies. I tried many recipes but couldn't match the chewy texture and chocolatey richness. When I started working at the Inn at Thorn Hill years later, the outgoing pastry chef, McKaella, has this in her recipe file. It's really amazing. You really need to chill the dough on this one or it will be impossible to shape and roll in sugar before baking. It will be worth the wait. If you leave it in the fridge too long, it will get quite hard. I find I need to set a timer on busy days, so I don't forget about it.

Ingredient	Home	Metric
Bittersweet chocolate	1 ½ C	255g
Flour	1 ¼ C	175g
Cocoa powder, sifted	½ C	45g
Baking powder	1t	4g
Salt	¼ t	2g
Unsalted Butter, softened	8T (1 stick)	114g
Brown sugar	1 1/3 C	267g
Eggs	2	100g
Vanilla extract	1t	5g
Milk	3T	45g

Powdered sugar for rolling

Preheat oven to 375°F
Yield about 24 cookies

Method
In a bowl, whisk together the cocoa, flour, salt, and baking powder. Set aside
Melt chocolate, either in a double boiler or in a microwave. If using the microwave, cook 30 seconds at a time and stir every time to ensure it melts slowly. Set aside to cool.
Cream the butter and brown sugar until fluffy. If you are mixing this by hand this task will seem impossible, as there is more sugar than butter. Mix with a wooden spoon until it gets to the point where the butter is incorporated with the sugar.
Add the eggs and vanilla and beat until the mixture is light.
Add the melted chocolate, stirring until smooth
Add half of the dry ingredients and mix until smooth
Stir in the milk

Add the remainder of the dry ingredients and mix until fully incorporated. The dough will be thick.
Chill 1-2 hours.

Scoop the dough with a black handled disher or use a spoon to measure ping pong sized pieces of dough. Round the dough.

Roll in powdered sugar before baking.

Bake on a parchment lined sheet pan for 10-12 minutes. The cookies should look puffed, and matte in the cracks. They should feel soft yet firm to the touch when pressed gently on the top.

Double Chocolate Nut Cookies
This is another recipe I found in McKaella's recipe book when I worked at the Inn at Thorn Hill. They are a bit of a fuss to make but they are incredibly rich and delicious. The dough holds up really well in the freezer, so keep it there in pre portioned amounts and bake them straight from the freezer.

Ingredient	Home	Metric
Bittersweet chocolate	4 C	680g
Butter, unsalted	1 C (2 sticks)	228g
Sugar	2 ¼ C	450g
Eggs	6	300g
Instant espresso powder	1T	7g
Vanilla extract	1T	15g
Flour	1 1/3 C	187g
Baking powder	¾ t	3g
Salt	1 ½ t	8g
White chocolate chips	2 ¾ C	467g
Walnuts	2 ¼ C	257g
Pecans	2 ¼ C	257g

Preheat oven to 350°F
Yield about 78 cookies

Method
Melt the chocolate and butter on a double boiler and set aside.
In a mixer fitted with a whisk attachment, mix the eggs, and sugar until light and fluffy, about 5 minutes.
Add the vanilla extract and instant espresso powder.

Add the chocolate mixture and mix on low speed to combine.
Switch to the paddle attachment.
Add the flour, baking powder, and salt and mix until smooth.
Add in the white chocolate chips, walnuts, and pecans.
Chill the dough for 1 hour.
Scoop the dough with a black handled disher or spoon the dough into ping pong ball sized pieces and shape into rounds.
Bake for 10-12 minutes. If baking from the freezer, bake a few minutes longer.

Coconut Macaroons

I have made many variations of coconut macaroons in my career. Some are even cooked over a double boiler. These cookies take patience waiting for the egg whites to whip completely, but it is worth it.   They are light and fluffy and have been a staple in our rotating cookie lineup since 2010 when we opened.

Ingredients	Home	Metric
Egg whites, fresh	3	85g
Sugar	¾ C	148g
Sweetened flaked coconut	1 -14 oz bag (3 ¼ C)	396g
Vanilla extract	2t	6g

Preheat oven to 350 F
Yield about 24

Method
In a mixer fitted with the whisk attachment, whip egg whites on a medium speed until foamy looking, about 2 minutes.
Add the sugar
Whip on high speed until a stiff, shiny meringue forms, about 15 minutes.
This will feel like it takes forever, so be patient!
Fold in coconut and vanilla.
Scoop macaroons with a black handled scoop or spoon golf ball sized portions of dough onto a parchment lined sheet pan.
Bake about 18 minutes or until evenly golden brown.

Chocolate Coconut Macaroons

How can you make coconut macaroons even better? Make a chocolate version. So good.

Ingredients	Home	Metric
Egg whites, fresh	3	342
Sugar	¾ C	518g
Sweetened flaked coconut	1 -14 oz bag (3 ¼ C)	906g
Vanilla extract	2t	15g
Semi-sweet chocolate		612
Unsweetened Chocolate		290g

Preheat oven to 350 F
Yield about 24

Method
In a double boiler, melt the two chocolates together.
Set aside to cool.
In a mixer fitted with the whisk attachment, whip egg whites on a medium speed until foamy looking, about 2 minutes.
Add the sugar
Whip on high speed until a stiff, shiny meringue forms, about 15 minutes.
This will feel like it takes forever, so be patient!
Fold in the melted chocolate.
Fold in coconut and vanilla.
Scoop macaroons with a black handled scoop or spoon golf ball sized portions of dough onto a parchment lined sheet pan.
Bake about 18 minutes or until evenly golden brown.

Biscotti

I love making up biscotti for the holidays. You can make up a few batches and mix & match them in gift bags. I like to make a variety, from classic varieties like anise and almond, to a more adventurous variety with pistachios, cranberries, and just a hint of black pepper. Biscotti hold well over a longer period of time so you can make them ahead. The dough can be made ahead and frozen after the first bake. Take the logs out of the freezer and allow them to thaw, then slice and bake as needed. Flavors can also easily be substituted. Don't like almonds? Use pecans or hazelnuts instead. Adverse to anise? Sub in vanilla extract instead. Also, if you find biscotti dough sticky to work with, it is okay to flour your hands and table lightly. Chilling the dough can help reduce the stickiness when shaping into logs too.

Almond Biscotti

These are the bakery biscotti we used to make all of the time. We stopped making them as an everyday cookie because the large batches can be so time consuming. They are crunchy, but not too hard. If the dough feels a bit sticky, it's okay to use a little flour on the dough. We always use sliced almonds since we have them on hand, but it'll work equally well with whole almonds.

Ingredient	Home	Metric
Unsalted butter, soft	1 stick	114g
Sugar	1 C	198g
Eggs	2	100g
Flour	1 ¾ C	223g
Baking powder	½ t	2g
Baking soda	½ t	3g
Salt	pinch	2g
Almonds, sliced	1 ½ C	129g
Almond Extract	½ t	5g
Vanilla Extract	1 t	5g

Preheat oven to 375F
Yield about 20

Method

Cream the butter and sugar until light.
Add the eggs and mix on medium speed until light.
Add the baking powder, baking soda, and extracts.
Stir to combine.
Add the flour and mix until it becomes a smooth dough.
Mix in the almonds. The dough will be soft.

Sprinkle some flour on your countertop.
Divide the dough into two portions.

Shape the dough into two logs 12" long.

Flour your hands as necessary to keep them from sticking.

Place the logs on a parchment lined sheet pan.

Alternatively, you may wrap the logs in plastic wrap and store them in the refrigerator a few days or in the freezer up to one month.

Bake 20-30 minutes until the tops feel springy when pressed.

Allow the biscotti to cool until they can be handled.

Slice the biscotti in ¾" slices and return them to the pan.

Bake again for 10 minutes.

Flip the biscotti and bake an additional 10 minutes.

Chocolate Pecan Biscotti

I love chocolate biscotti. I like the bitterness of the cocoa and the burst of chocolate from a chip now and then. While the nuts make these biscotti delicious, I will sometimes add in some orange zest or a teaspoon of cinnamon to the dough too. This recipe was adapted from the one in *Pastries* from Standard Baking Company in Portland, Maine. It is more of an American style biscotti as it contains butter – it will be a little crumblier and a little less crunchy.

Ingredient	Home	Metric
Flour	3C	420g
Cocoa, sifted	¾ C plus 1 T	72g
Baking soda	2t	10g
Salt	1 ½ t	8g
Butter	1 stick (8T)	114g
Sugar	1 ½ C	300g
Eggs	3 ea	150g
Pecans	1C	114g
Chocolate Chunks	1 ¼ C	212g

Preheat oven to 375F
Yield about 30 cookies

Method

In a bowl, whisk together the flour, cocoa, baking soda and salt.

In a separate bowl or in a mixer fitted with a paddle attachment, cream the butter and sugar until light and fluffy

On low speed, add the eggs one at a time

One they are all added, mix until fully combined

Add the flour mixture a little at a time until all ingredients are incorporated.
Add the pecans and chocolate chunks
Divide the dough into two equal pieces.
Roll into a log 12"
Press down to shape 14" x 3" x ½ " thick

Bake 20 mins

Reduce oven to 325
Slice to ¾ " thickness

Bake 12 minutes more.
Flip the biscotti over and baker 12 minutes more.

Pistachio Cranberry Biscotti

Pistachios are a great addition to biscotti. They add a bright green color, and their toasty flavor is a great accompaniment to tea or coffee. The black pepper adds a little savory note that isn't overwhelming. If it doesn't appeal to you it won't hurt to leave it out.

Ingredient	Home	Metric
Unsalted butter, soft	1 stick	114g
Sugar	1 C	198g
Eggs	2	100g
Flour	1 ¾ C	223g
Baking powder	½ t	2g
Baking soda	½ t	3g
Salt	pinch	2g
Pistachios	¾ C	86g
Dried Cranberries	¾ C	128g
Black Pepper	1t	8g
Almond Extract	½ t	5g
Vanilla Extract	1 t	5g

Preheat oven to 375F
Yield about 24

Method

Cream the butter and sugar until light.
Add the eggs and cream.
Add the baking powder, baking soda, black pepper, and extracts.
Stir to combine.
Add the flour and mix until it becomes a smooth dough.
Mix in the pistachios and dried cranberries. The dough will be soft.

Sprinkle some flour on your countertop.
Divide the dough into two portions.
Shape the dough into two logs 12" long.
Flour your hands as necessary to keep them from sticking.
Place the logs on a parchment lined sheet pan.
Alternatively, you may wrap the logs in plastic wrap and store them in the refrigerator a few days or in the freezer up to one month.
Bake 20-30 minutes until the tops feel springy when pressed.
Allow the biscotti to cool until they can be handled.
Slice the biscotti in ¾" slices and return them to the pan.
Bake again for 10 minutes.
Flip the biscotti and bake an additional 10 minutes.

Anise Biscotti

These are the biscotti of my youth. We always seemed to have them at the holidays or at any large family gathering. I love snacking on these biscotti any time, but especially with coffee at breakfast.

Ingredient	Home	Metric
Oil	½ C	112g
Sugar	1C	200g
Eggs	3	150g
Anise Extract	1T	15g
Flour	3 ¼ C	396g
Baking powder	1T	10g

Preheat oven to 375°F
Yield about 24 cookies

Method

In a medium bowl, combine oil, eggs, sugar, and anise extract until well blended. Add flour and baking powder, stir into the egg mixture to form a heavy dough.

Divide the dough into two pieces. Form each piece into a log about 12 inches long. Place roll onto a cookies sheet lined with parchment paper. Flatten the log until it is about ½" thick.

Bake for 20-30 minutes, until the cookie logs are fully cooked and feel springy to the touch.

When the cookies logs are cool enough to handle, slice each one into ½" slices. Return cookies to the baking sheet, cut side up.

Bake for 6-10 minutes, then flip them over to the other side and return to the oven for another 6-10 minutes.

Gingerbread Biscotti

These biscotti are a nice mix up in holiday gift box. There biscotti are more like a traditional Italian biscotti in the at they are made without fat. Fatless biscotti are going to be crunchier, and thus better for dunking in a cup of tea or coffee. This recipe makes two large logs of biscotti. The two logs can be baked together on a sheet pan but will likely touch. The dough can easily be divided into four smaller logs instead, and would produce a smaller biscotti, similar to what the other biscotti recipes call for. Making smaller cookies will also shorten the baking times for both the loaf of dough and the individual cookies. Personally, I like the option of the larger biscotti as they make a grander presentation in a package.

Ingredient	Home	Metric
Flour	4C	560g
Ginger, ground	4t	20g
Baking powder	2 ½ t	9g
Cinnamon	2T	30g
Salt	1t	6g
Nutmeg	½ t	3g
Baking soda	½ t	2g
Pecans, chopped	2 ½ C	285g
Dried apricots, chopped	1 ½ C	192g
Brown sugar	2C	400g
Eggs	4	200g
Molasses	½ C	168g
Orange Zest	1T	6g

Preheat oven to 350 F
Yield about 30 large biscotti

Method

In a bowl, stir together the dry ingredients (flour, spices, baking powder, baking soda, salt) to combine.

In a mixer fitted with a paddle, combine eggs, molasses, orange zest. Mix until combined.

Add dry ingredients to the wet ingredients.
Add the pecans and chopped apricots.
Mix on low speed until a dough comes together.

Divide the dough into two logs and shape to be about 10 inches by 3 inches.

Place the logs onto a parchment lined sheet pan and flatten slightly.

Bake 20-30 minutes or until the dough feels springy when touched.

Let cool.

When the cookies logs are cool enough to handle, slice each one into ½" slices. Return cookies to the baking sheet, cut side up.

Bake for 10-15 minutes on each side.

Bibliography

Standard Baking Co. Pastries, Allison Pray and Tara Reid, Downeast Publications, 2012

Sweet Maria's Italian Cookie Tray, Maria Bruscino Sanchez, St. Martin's Press, 1997.

King Arthur Flour Cookie Companion, King Arthur Baking Company, The Countryman Press, 2021

The Professional Pastry Chef, Bo Frieberg, Wiley, 2005

Baker's Notes Issue No. 4, Scratch Baking Company, 2012/2013

The Bread Baker's Pocket Companion, Andrew Janjigian, Scout Books, 2022

www.ingramcontent.com/pod-product-compliance
Lightning Source LLC
Chambersburg PA
CBHW072202090426
42740CB00012B/2361